KIDNEYS

Shannon Caster

PowerKiDS press

New York

To my science teachers, who always allowed me to explore

Published in 2010 by The Rosen Publishing Group, Inc.
29 East 21st Street, New York, NY 10010

First Edition

Editor: Joanne Randolph
Book Design: Greg Tucker
Layout Design: Kate Laczynski
Photo Researcher: Jessica Gerweck

Photo Credits: Cover, pp. 6 (inset), 13, 17 (inset), 18, 21 Shutterstock.com; pp. 5, 6, 9, 17, 18 (inset) 3D4Medical.com/Getty Images; p. 10 3D Clinic/Getty Images; p. 13 DEA Picture Library/Getty Images; p. 14 Nucleus Medical Art, Inc./Getty Images.

Library of Congress Cataloging-in-Publication Data

Caster, Shannon.
 Kidneys / Shannon Caster.
    p. cm. — (Body works)
 Includes index.
 ISBN 978-1-4358-9372-6 (library binding) — ISBN 978-1-4358-9832-5 (pbk.) —
 ISBN 978-1-4358-9833-2 (6-pack)
 1. Kidneys—Physiology—Juvenile literature. I. Title.
 QP249.C37 2010
 612.4'63—dc22
                                    2009034733

5845

Manufactured in the United States

CPSIA Compliance Information: Batch #WW10PK: For Further Information contact Rosen Publishing, New York, New York at 1-800-237-9932

Contents

The Body's Filter   4

Blood and the Renal Arteries   7

Tiny Filters at Work   8

Leaving the Kidneys   11

Hold On: The Bladder   12

On the Way Out   15

A Balancing Act   16

Kidneys and Hormones   19

Kidneys and Calcium   20

Kidney Trouble   22

Glossary   23

Index   24

Web Sites   24

The Body's Filter

The kidneys are two bean-shaped **organs** located near your spine just about where your rib cage ends. The kidneys have an important job to do in your body. They filter, or separate out, waste and extra water from your blood. Then the kidneys check your blood and add back missing salts or water before sending the blood to the rest of the body.

Every day your kidneys filter around 200 quarts (200 L) of blood. Only 2 quarts (2 L) of waste will leave the kidneys in the form of **urine**.

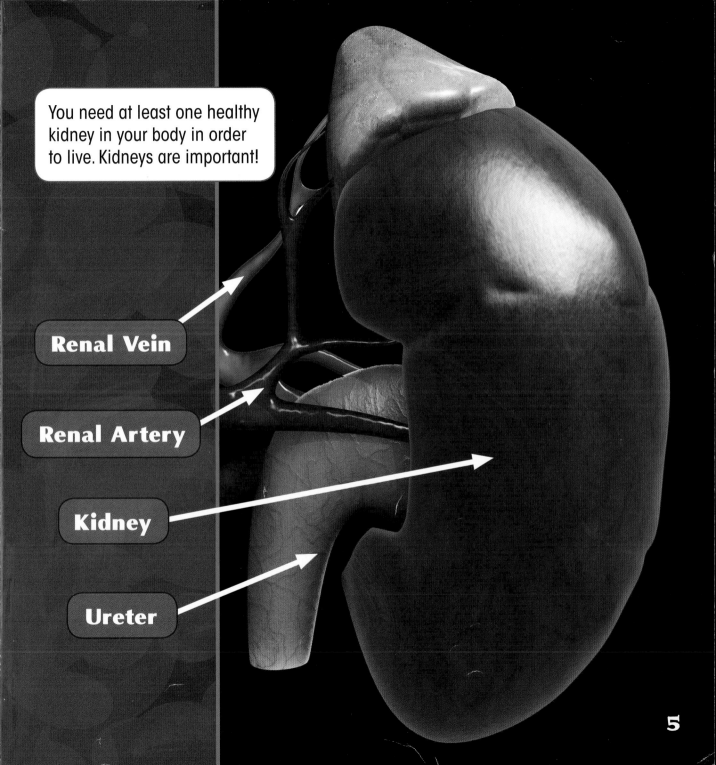

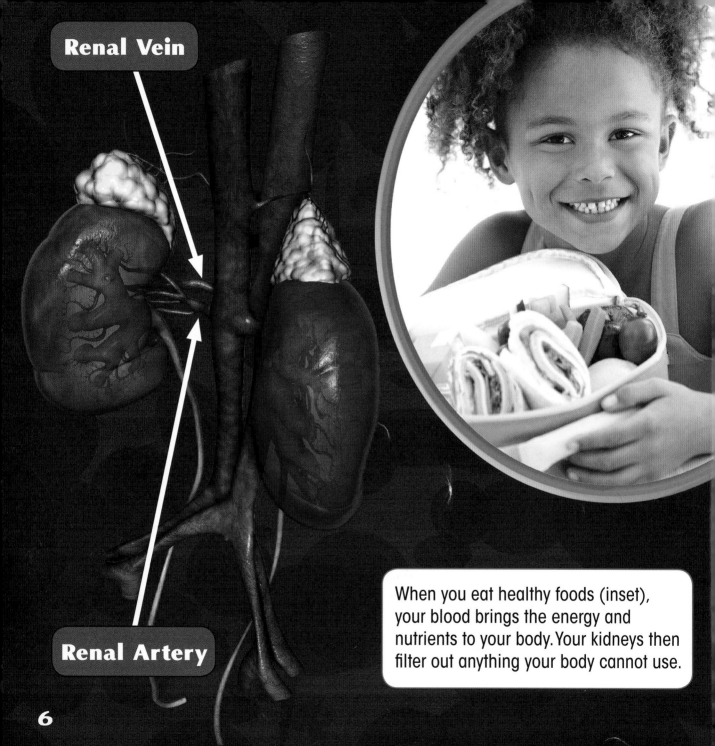

Renal Vein

Renal Artery

When you eat healthy foods (inset), your blood brings the energy and nutrients to your body. Your kidneys then filter out anything your body cannot use.

Blood and the Renal Arteries

One of the jobs of your blood is to carry food energy to your cells, **tissues**, and organs. After your body uses the power from the food, the waste, or leftover matter, is carried away by your blood. These waste products collect and build up in your blood until your kidneys can filter them out.

The renal arteries are the major **blood vessels** that bring blood filled with waste to your kidneys. One renal artery enters your left kidney and one enters your right kidney. Once the renal arteries carry blood to the kidneys, filtering can begin.

Tiny Filters at Work

There are more than a million small filtering units, or parts, called nephrons in each kidney. The nephrons act as small cleaning and **recycling** centers.

Blood enters a tiny vessel in the nephron called a glomerulus (gluh-MER-yuh-lus). In the glomerulus, extra sugars, salts, and water are filtered out along with other waste. This waste matter enters a tube called a tubule. The tubule is the recycling center. Any sugars, salts, and water that can be reused by the body are returned to the bloodstream. Anything that cannot be reused keeps moving through the tubule as urine.

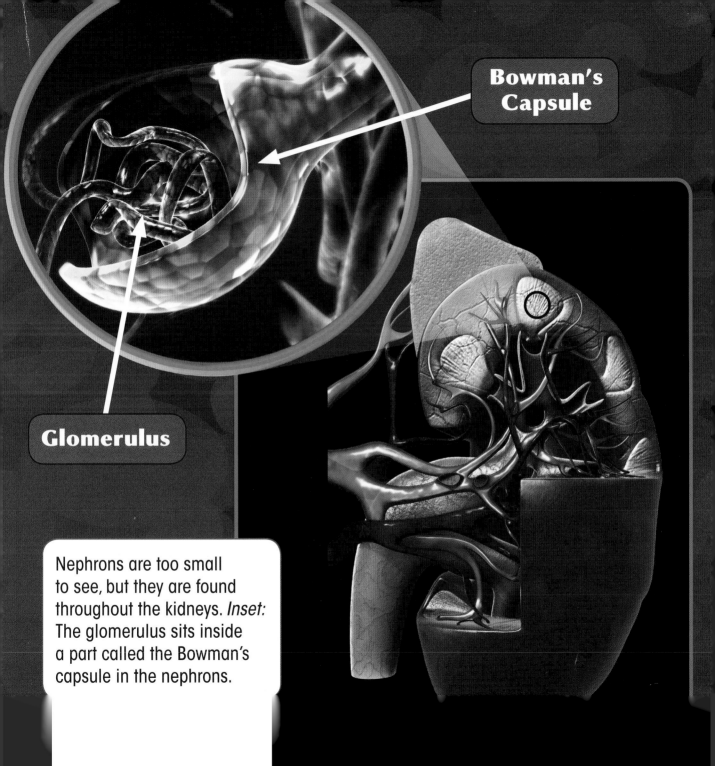

Bowman's Capsule

Glomerulus

Nephrons are too small to see, but they are found throughout the kidneys. *Inset:* The glomerulus sits inside a part called the Bowman's capsule in the nephrons.

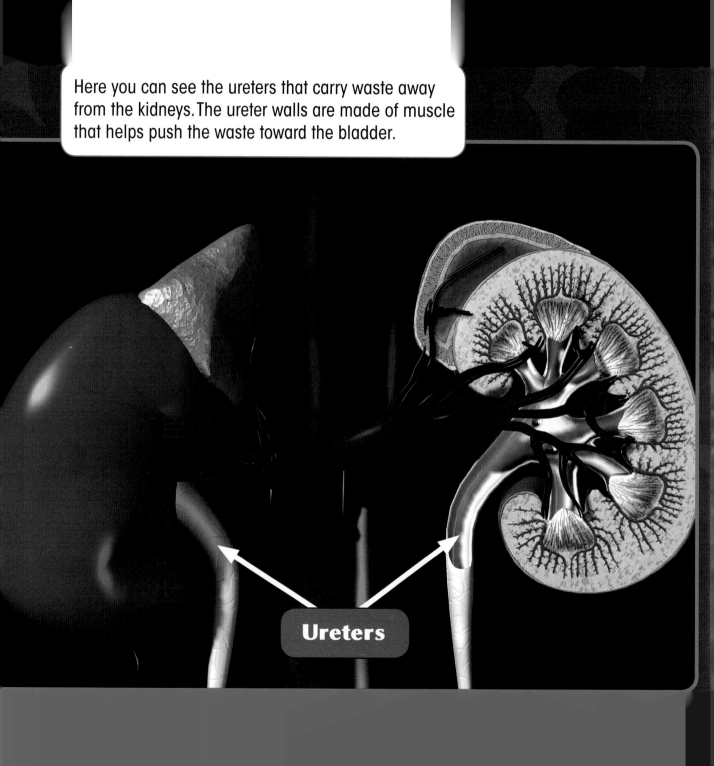

Here you can see the ureters that carry waste away from the kidneys. The ureter walls are made of muscle that helps push the waste toward the bladder.

Ureters

Leaving the Kidneys

Urine leaves your kidneys through two small tubes called ureters. Each ureter is about 8 to 10 inches (20–25 cm) long and connects your kidneys to your bladder. Since your kidneys are always filtering blood, small amounts of urine are always released, or let out, into the ureters.

Small muscles in the ureter wall contract, or squeeze, to push the urine away from the kidneys. This prevents urine from remaining in the ureters and backing up into the kidneys. To keep the urine flow moving, the ureters squeeze out small amounts of urine to the bladder four to six times a minute.

Hold On: The Bladder ———

The bladder is a balloon-shaped organ located in the lower part of your **abdomen**. Like a balloon, the bladder grows bigger, or expands, as urine collects there. Small muscles around the opening of the bladder contract, or get smaller, to keep urine from dripping out while the bladder is filling up.

When the bladder is full, it becomes round and your body sends a signal to your brain that you need to use the bathroom. Once you are ready to use the bathroom, the bladder contracts and the muscles keeping the bladder shut relax and open. This allows urine to leave the bladder all at once.

The bladder, shown from the top here, holds on to urine until it gets full. This lets you play and do other activities without needing to use the bathroom all the time.

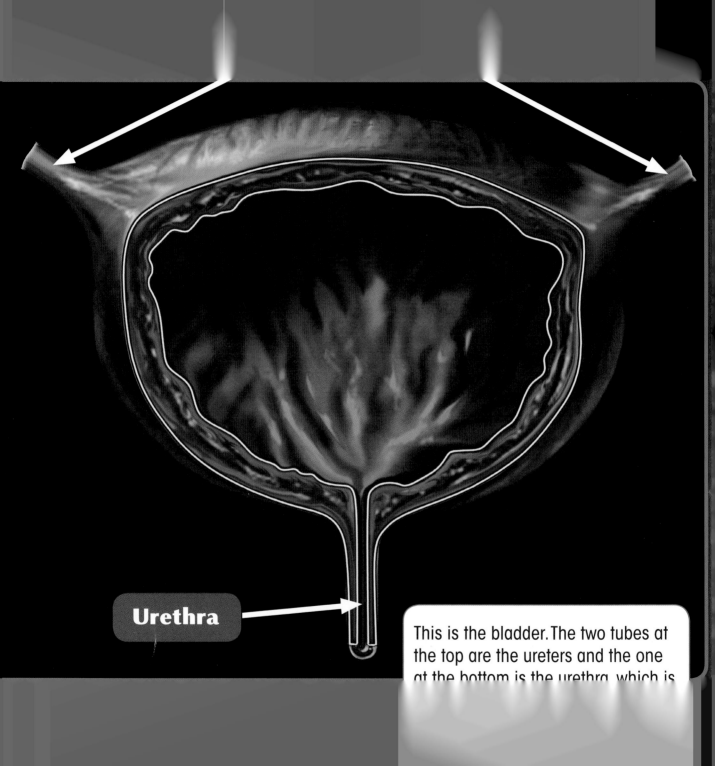

Urethra

This is the bladder. The two tubes at the top are the ureters and the one at the bottom is the urethra, which is

On the Way Out

The journey your urine takes as it leaves your body is almost over. When the bladder opens and urine leaves, it enters one last tube, called the urethra. The urethra connects the bladder to an opening that lets the urine leave the body.

The urine leaving your body is very concentrated, or filled, with waste. This waste makes your urine **acidic**. Therefore, tiny **glands** inside the urethra wall secrete, or give off, a sticky matter called mucus. This mucus keeps the urethra from being hurt by the acid in the urine that is leaving your body.

A Balancing Act

The kidneys do more than filter waste. They help your body keep itself in homeostasis (ho-me-oh-STAY-sis). Homeostasis is a state in which the body is in balance and every part of it is working together.

One way the kidneys help is by keeping track of how much water is in your blood. If your blood has too little water, your kidneys do not send as much water out. The body needs water to help break down food. It also needs water to keep your body from getting too hot or too cold. The kidneys also make sure there is the right amount of salt in your blood. Salts help messages cross from your **nerves** to your muscles.

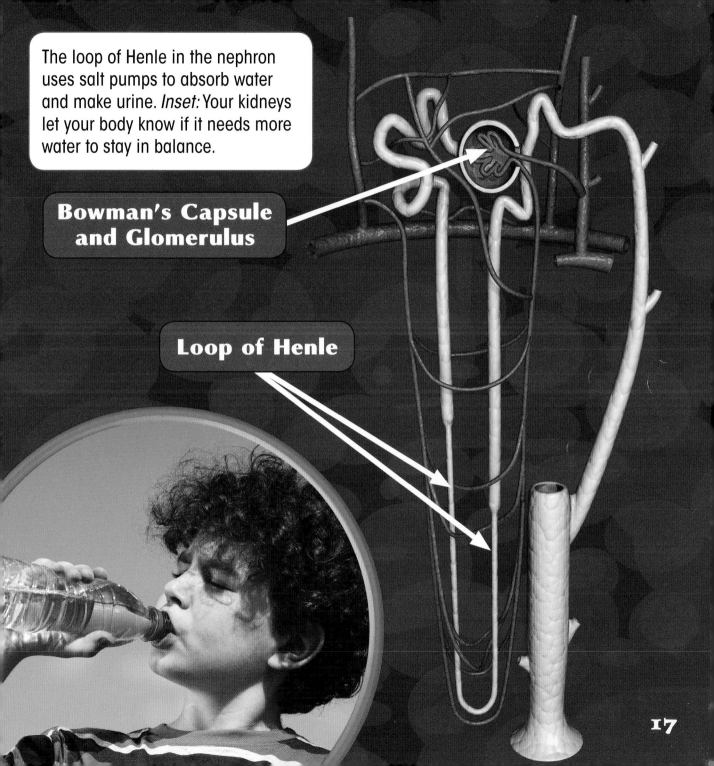

The loop of Henle in the nephron uses salt pumps to absorb water and make urine. *Inset:* Your kidneys let your body know if it needs more water to stay in balance.

Bowman's Capsule and Glomerulus

Loop of Henle

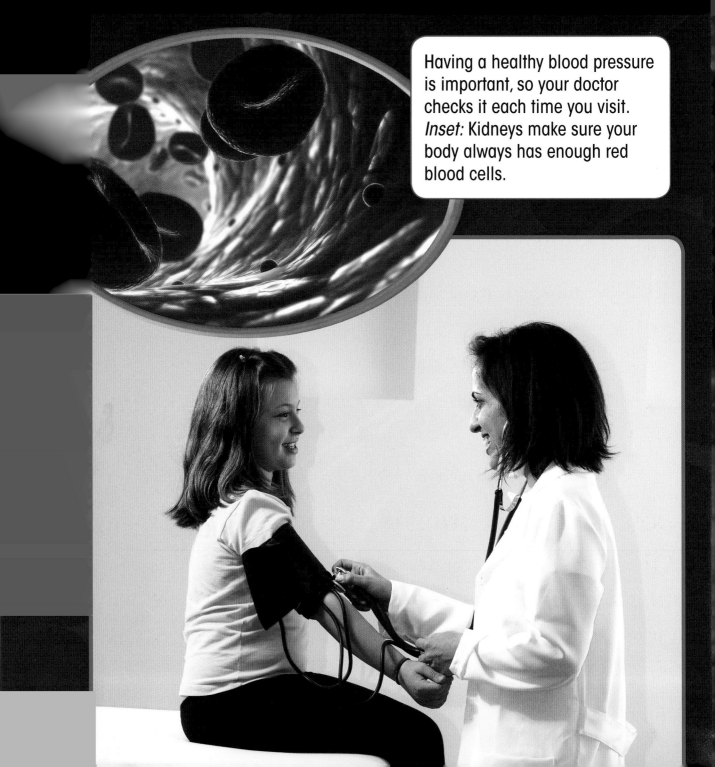

Having a healthy blood pressure is important, so your doctor checks it each time you visit. *Inset:* Kidneys make sure your body always has enough red blood cells.

Kidneys and Hormones

Another way the kidneys help with homeostasis is by releasing **hormones**. The kidneys release a hormone that controls how many red blood cells are produced. Red blood cells live for only about four months before breaking down. Since red blood cells carry oxygen to the body, you need a steady supply to live.

The kidneys also release a hormone that controls **blood pressure**. If your blood has too little salt, your blood pressure drops. To fix the problem, your kidneys release a hormone to hold on to more salt in the blood. This balances the body and returns your blood pressure to normal.

Kidneys and Calcium

Your body needs certain vitamins and minerals, which we get from food, to stay healthy. Vitamin D is used to help your body grow and develop strong bones. The kidneys help turn vitamin D in the blood into a hormone called calcitriol. Calcitriol helps the body and bones absorb, or take in and use, calcium from food.

Phosphorus is a mineral the body needs to stay healthy, too. However, too much phosphorus keeps the bones from absorbing calcium. The kidneys help keep the right balance between calcium and phosphorus by filtering out what the body does not need.

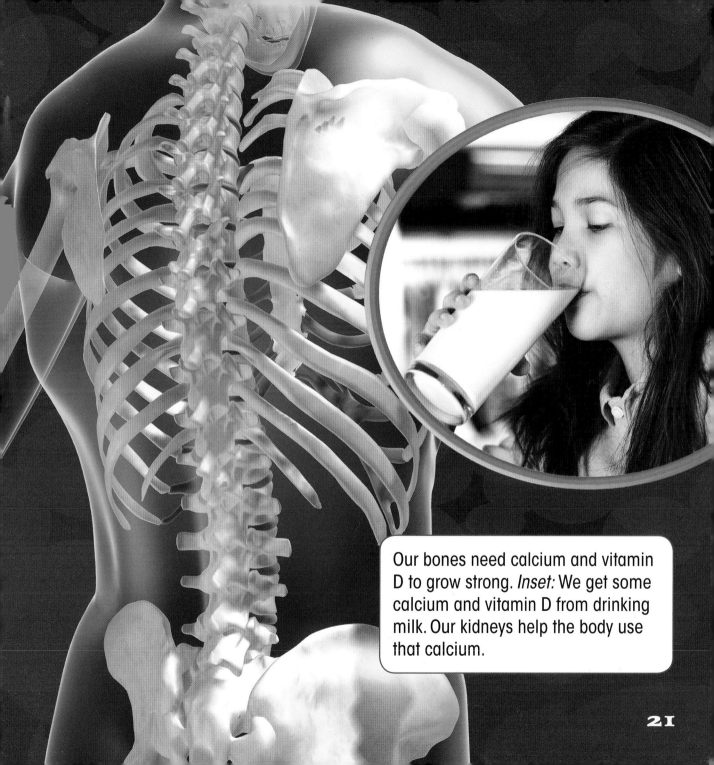

Our bones need calcium and vitamin D to grow strong. *Inset:* We get some calcium and vitamin D from drinking milk. Our kidneys help the body use that calcium.

Kidney Trouble

Sometimes the kidneys do not work as they should. If the kidneys are not working, wastes can build up in the blood and hurt the body.

Humans can live with just one kidney. However, if both kidneys stop working, a person needs help to stay alive. Some people may need dialysis (dy-AL-uh-sis). In dialysis, a machine does the work of the kidneys and filters the blood. A person with kidney trouble may need to receive a kidney transplant. During a kidney transplant, a specially trained doctor takes out the bad kidney and puts in a healthy kidney from another person.

Glossary

abdomen (AB-duh-mun) The lower belly.

acidic (A-SIH-dik) Having to do with something that breaks down matter faster than water does.

blood pressure (BLUD PREH-shur) The force created in the veins by the heart pumping blood through the body.

blood vessels (BLUD VEH-sulz) Narrow tubes in the body through which blood flows.

glands (GLANDZ) Parts of the body that produce matter to help with the body's jobs.

hormones (HOR-mohnz) Matter in your body that controls what happens in different parts of the body.

nerves (NERVZ) Groups of fibers, or threads, that carry messages between the brain and other parts of the body.

organs (OR-genz) Parts inside the body that do jobs.

recycling (ree-SY-kling) Using things again instead of getting rid of them.

tissues (TIH-shooz) Matter that forms the parts of living things.

urine (YUR-un) A liquid, or waterlike, waste made by the body.

Index

A
abdomen, 12

B
blood, 4, 7–8, 11, 16, 19–20, 22
blood pressure, 19
bloodstream, 8
blood vessels, 7
body, 4, 7–8, 12, 15–16, 19–20

C
cells, 7, 19

E
energy, 7

G
glands, 15
glomerulus, 8

H
hormone(s), 19–20

N
nephrons, 8
nerves, 16

O
organ(s), 4, 7, 12

R
rib cage, 4

S
salt(s), 4, 8, 16, 19
spine, 4
sugars, 8

T
tissues, 7
tubule, 8

U
ureters, 11
urine, 4, 8, 11–12, 15

W
waste(s), 4, 7–8, 15–16, 22
water, 4, 8, 16

Web Sites

Due to the changing nature of Internet links, PowerKids Press has developed an online list of Web sites related to the subject of this book. This site is updated regularly. Please use this link to access the list:
www.powerkidslinks.com/hybw/kidney/